Werewolf Club Rules

Joseph Coelho

For Nana - Who gave me her dictionary
For Dada - who told me stories

Versions of the following poems were published in *Read me at School*,
edited by Gaby Morgan, Macmillan Children's Books 2009
Hamster! Hamster!
Miss Flotsam
An A* from Miss Coo
Make it bigger, Eileen!

A version of the following poem was published in *The Works 6*,
edited by Pie Corbett, Macmillan Children's Books 2007
If all the world were paper

JANETTA OTTER-BARRY BOOKS

Text copyright © Joseph Coelho 2014
Illustrations copyright © John O'Leary 2014

First published in Great Britain and in the USA in 2014 by
Frances Lincoln Children's Books,
74-77 White Lion Street, London N1 9PF
www.franceslincoln.com

A CIP catalogue record for this book is available on request.

ISBN 978-1-84780-452-5

Printed and bound by CPI Group (UK) Ltd, Croydon.

Werewolf Club
Rules

Poems by
Joseph Coelho

Illustrations by
John O'Leary

F

FRANCES LINCOLN
CHILDREN'S BOOKS

Contents

Hamster! Hamster!

We've got a hamster in our class,
as brown as toffee.
He's so sweet, so cute,
with chubby cheeks
for storing nuts and fruit.
He sips from a water bottle
strapped to his cage,
like a little baby!
Awww, he's soooooo cute.
He's got these darling little paws
like a doll's hands,
and a sweet, cute, tiny little tail
like a little piece of spaghetti!
Awwwww, he is soooooo deliciously cute.

One day I put my finger up to his cage,
and he sniffed it with a nose
like a chocolate-chip button
and he... BIT ME!

We've got a hamster in our class,
as brown as a bog.
He is so mean, so horrible,
with fat cheeks
for storing pupils' fingers.
He sucks at a water bottle
strapped to his cage,
like a greedy rat!
Errr, he's soooooo disgusting.
He's got these vicious claws
as terrible as a tiger's,
and a long, wiggerly, squiggerly tail
as scaly as a snake!
ARRRRR
he is soooooo perfectly horrid.

Einstein

Albert Einstein
Had an explosive mind
And hair to make people scared
But none can ignore the genius of E=MC2

Prove it

"Water's got skin," I said.
"Prove it," suggested Miss Irwin.
"Come here and look!" I said.
"Prove it," challenged Miss Irwin.

"Lee can see it, Miss, can't you, Lee?"
"Prove it."
"But it's right there."
"Prove it."
"On top of the tank! A layer like skin,
different from the rest."
"Prove it."

"Ink sits on the surface, it sits on the skin!"
"Well done... and..."
"When you fill a glass to the edge,
the skin stops it from spilling."
"Brilliant... and..."

"If I put a paper clip on top,
the skin stops it from sinking."
"Excellent... and..."

"If water's got a skin, Miss,
then why can't it be cut?
And why can I not peel it?
And hang the water-skin up?"

Miss Irwin gave a smile,
impressed by all my questions,
then gave an incredible lesson
about a thing called water tension.

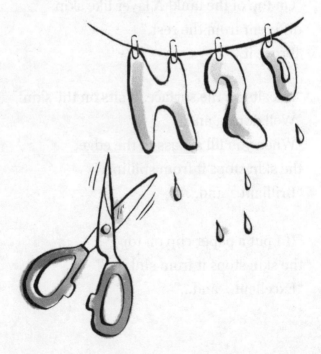

Miss Flotsam

Miss Flotsam was my reception teacher.
She had travelled the world.
Brown hair turned golden
under distant suns,
clothes carrying colours
from countless corners of continents.

When my mother's face spilled
a gush of adolescent tears
at the school gates,
Miss Flotsam soaked up the drops
in Peruvian alpaca,
caught splashes
in Himalayan singing bowls,
let sobs fall on Indonesian Gamelans.

Miss Flotsam had flown
through air pockets in jumbo jets,
sailed the seven seas
in opposite directions,
cycled through cyclones
with dengue fever,
soothed mothers
when their hearts heaved.

When the bully punched me
for being too brown,
Miss Flotsam glared at him
with an eye that could turn fists
into begging bowls.

When my mother was late,
the chairs upturned on the desks,
Miss Flotsam read to me
stories of imperfect families
and unexpected heroes.

When I dozed in class
Miss Flotsam let me sleep
through maths,
through lunch,
through the tuk-tuk traffic,
through the home-time bell.

When I was naughty
Miss Flotsam told me off,
asked of the disasters
destroying my home
and placed sandbags around my lies.

Miss Flotsam had climbed peaks
circled by vultures,
waded rivers with unseen bottoms,
bought ugly fruits
in dusty languages
in foreign markets,
spoke to parents
in dialects they could understand,
sang to pupils
in rhythms they could bear.

Weights on a pole

MissIrwinTaughtUsScienceByPuttingAPlasticBagOnABroom
HandleAndLayingItAcrossTheTopsOfTwoChairs

We

Added

Large Metal Weights

Until The Bag Reached its Capacity And...

S

L

P

I

T

Bug poem

Hanging from a silken web,
landing on my sister's head!
A hairy bug.

Living under the toilet seat,
smelling like my brother's feet!
A stinky bug.

Wearing lipstick and make-up,
landing on my mum's teacup.
A lady bug.

Drawing pictures without a care,
sitting in my grandad's chair.
A doodle bug.

Always asleep and in a doze,
curled up in my grandma's clothes.
A snug bug.

On my head and under my hat
I pulled on too hard and it went splat!
A dead bug.

You look like a rainbow

Ben dressed himself for the first time
in yellows, greens and browns.
He looked so bright and colourful,
his mother glared with a frown!

"Did you run through a painting?
Did you dress yourself at night?
You can't go to school like that, son,
you'll give your teachers a fright."

"I'll delight all that pass me
with my hues of spring-time fire.
The entire school will be charmed
by my multi-coloured attire."

Mother saw he could not be stopped
as he mis-matched his boots, scarf and coat.
Mother put on her grey jacket,
fastened her grey scarf to her throat.

All beamed at Ben as he splashed
in boots gold and aquamarine.
All gasped as he gathered up leaves
with gloves rose and tangerine.

The school gathered for assembly,
Mother couldn't help but stare.
The teachers were draped in colours,
with jewels woven into their hair!

Parents arrived with their children
dressed in rainbows, dapples and streaks.
Mother looked at her grey clothes.
Mother's eyes started to leak.

First came a child with a sari
of the deepest gingery brown,
a teacher with a dawn-dust scarf,
they wrapped Mother round and round.

Mother smiled in her fineries
as more was added to her style.
All said, "How pretty you look, dear."
She blushed like a spring-bathed isle.

Now Mother and Ben are strolling
in umber and harlequin sun,
dressed in the colours of daring,
her love lit by her marbled son.

Kiss petals onto my eyes

Lullaby me, cuddle-dry me.
Pat me down
with hands that have sponged
every cut,
every bruise,
every fall.

Lullaby me, cuddle-dry me.
Squeeze all the water out of me
whenever tears fill me up
and make my eyes swim.

Lullaby me, cuddle-dry me.
Kiss my cheeks rosy
so they'll know no thorns.
Kiss petals onto my eyes
to bloom every vision.
Kiss sap into my ears
to honey all I hear.

Lullaby me, cuddle-dry me.
Play with my toes.
Toes that will dance with your smiles,
toes that will flee from your frowns,
toes that will...
run to you,
run to you,
run to you,
every time you call.

Lullaby me, cuddle-dry me.
Lace your fingers into mine,
weave your history into my hopes,
swaddle me in applause
and buffer me from hisses.

Lullaby me, cuddle-dry me.
Blow raspberries on my belly
because our laughs
scare darkness from night,
shake colours from dry palettes,
grow music where sounds have died.

Lullaby me, cuddle-dry me.
Breathe a breath we breathe together
until our scents
tingle on our taste buds,
mingle in our lungs,
linger in our thoughts.

Lullaby me, cuddle-dry me.
Place your hands on my head.
Place your lips on my cheeks.
Place your heart in my heart.

Siblings

Like the Three Musketeers
we were all for one.

Like the Three Blind Mice
we saw without looking.

Like the Three Bowls of Porridge
we were just right.

Like the Three Sisters
we were sad inside.

Like the Three Billy Goats Gruff
we feared the troll.

Like the Three Little Pigs
we longed for our own home.

Like the Three Wishes
we were never enough.

Dada's stories

Dada had stories from Calcutta
wrapped up in his big belly.
When he belched they would unravel.

Like the lady who gathered the water
in a pot by a river's melting thaw.
The villagers found her head rolling,
swiped off by a foul tiger's paw.

Dada had stories from Tibet
wound in the red flecks of his hair.
When he brushed it they'd fall out.

Like the pets hidden in his bedclothes
as he slept in the school at night,
found dead when he woke in the morning.
He'd slept holding them too tight.

Dada had stories from Goa,
locked in the tattoos on his arms.
When he moved they would speak.

Like the ponds he swam in when young,
with waters so murky and deep.
The weeds that grew within them,
that tugged as they wrapped round his feet.

Dada had stories from London
etched in the lines of his eyes.
When he cried they'd drip down.

Like the parties where he danced to Elvis,
shaking his hips and jet black hair,
the food cooked for the family,
the winnings he hoped to ensnare.

Dada had stories within him
that he took to his grave.
Stories that I try to honour,
that I recall when I need to be brave.

Puppy love

When puppies fall in love
they go on puppy dates
and buy each other bone-shaped treats
to treat their favourite mates.

When puppies fall in love
they fall head-over-paws
and gather each other flowers
that they deliver in their maws.

When puppies fall in love
their tails wag and twine
and they write puppy poetry
that rarely ever rhymes.

When puppies fall in love
their fur turns a shade of pink
and they cover themselves in perfume.
But puppy perfume stinks!

My puppy fell in love!
I should have acted quicker.
Now I have to pay
for my puppy's dates at dinner.

Simpson

We should have called him Smudge
due to the charcoal-like stain
on the tip of his nose.
Kissed by a miner.

We should have called him Silly
due to his runs into walls,
staggering on his paws.
The cat that lapped the beer.

We should have called him White Belly
due to his stomach patch of white fur,
sledding in snow on his tummy.
Winter's beast.

We should have called him Home
so he would have never lost his way.
A stray swallowed by London.
A corner-of-eye shadow on the street.

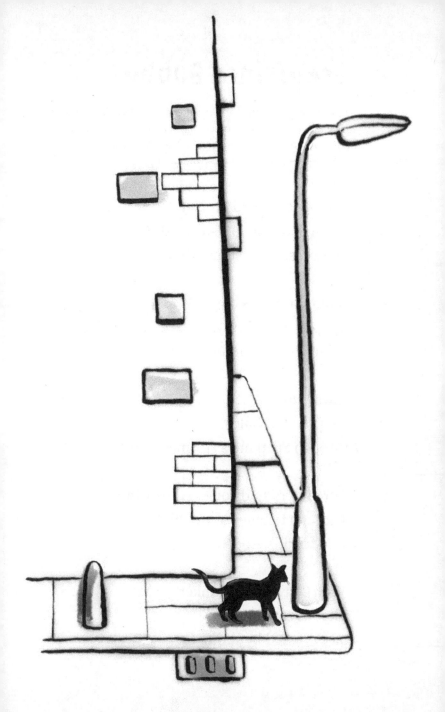

Greyfriars Bobby

*In Edinburgh during the 1800s there was a Skye Terrier who
accompanied his police-officer master wherever he went.
After his master died, Greyfriars Bobby kept guard on his
grave for 14 years, or so it is rumoured.*

John Gray would hunker
through Scotland's stormed streets,
face pressed by stone wind.

A mop-of-barks dog,
a yap-at-heels stray.
The copper's canine.

Always together,
come hail or halos,
through Scotland's stormed streets.

Through rain, through stone wind.
Through tongues of wet flint.
Two friends eroded.

John Gray would hunker
into his coughing,
face pressed by satin.

A sad-of-barks dog
found slumped on Gray's grave.
The copper's canine?

Alone he stays there,
come hail or halos
on Scotland's stormed stone.

Through rain, through inked wind,
through tales unfolding,
entombed by fiction.

JOHN GRAY
1814-1858

Wool

The wool of your jumper,
the leather of your shoe,
were all much happier
before skinned and put on you.

Tilly's tarts

Tilly's tarts were blooming brilliant
Petal pastry, sweet sap jam.
Huge in my small unfurling hands.

School dinner

A *slice* of gravy
A *spit* of jelly
A *smear* of custard
A *husk* of sausage
A *dribble* of beans
A sickly *sliver* of meat
A cold snotty *mush* of veg
A yellowed *rock* of sugar
A browning *mash* of fruit
A *lump* of milk
A *scab* of pizza.

A packed lunch please.

Joseph found these potatoes

Someone had thrown out the chip-maker.
Chucked away the mash-giver.
Discarded the jacket-wearer
because of the wrinkled skin,
because of all of the eyes.

I found it in the school garden,
a yard with one small almond tree
on a terrace of two tiers.
It lay in the Shetland-black dirt of the lowest level,
tendrils spreading around it like veins,
nodules sprouting
from this vein, from that vein,
a clustering of spuds to be boiled.

I next see them in a tank in the classroom,
King Edwards on fresh soil.

"Joseph found these potatoes outside.
We're going to see if they grow."

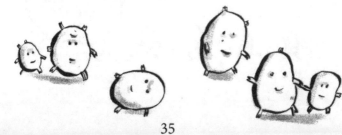

Little bit of food

A little bit of rice,
a little bit of pea,
on my plate
for my tea.

A little bit of jam,
a little bit of toast,
in the mornings
when I love it most.

A little bit of banger,
a little bit of mash,
in my belly
for a tasty bash.

A little bit of curry,
with a poppadom,
tastes great
but it burns my bum!

A little bit of *fufu*,
a little bit of stew,
eat with your fingers,
that's what we do.

A little bit of food,
on my plate,
eat it all up,
feeling great.

Conquer

Five children clasping mittens
could not hug the entire trunk.
Whole hands could hide in the folds of its bark.
James, the tallest boy in class,
could sit on a root,
his feet would not touch the ground.

Every classroom faced the playground,
every child could see the tree.
Leaves beckoning.
Conkers swelling.

As the bells rang
we'd march to the tree,
sticks in hand,
eyes fixed on the mace-like horse chestnuts.
Green spikes hungry to prick
our minds obsessed by the jewels within.

Halloween's crumble

The biggest berries are in the centre
of a tunnel of thorny bushes.
A shark gaping wide,
promising not to nip.

The juiciest berries dangle
from the barbed canes.
Savage whips,
swearing they won't mark.

The plumpest berries are out of reach,
boxed within sharp leaves.
A chest of swords,
vowing never to cut.

The best berries are in my tub.
Frogspawn, black beads, spider eyes,
wet and bleeding,
giving their word to please.

The sweetest berries
are in the crumble.
A rocky sandscape over a gory lake,
guaranteeing to be delicious.

Not just for Christmas

I've got a new puppy
all wrinkles and snout.
I run home from school
just to take him out.

I've got a new puppy
all fur and tail.
I take him for walks
come sunshine or hail.

I've got a new puppy
all head-pat and rub.
He doesn't like baths,
he leaps from the tub.

I've got a new puppy
all walks in the rain.
I must take him out,
this puppy's a pain.

I've got a new puppy
all poop and scoop.
I clean up his mess,
this puppy's a brute!

I've got a new puppy,
now my room's in a mess.
But he does lick my nose
when I feel a bit stressed.

I've got a new puppy,
some bad days, some sublime.
I'll take what he gives,
this puppy's all mine!

Timmy Tell-Tale

Timmy Tell-Tale
would tip tap on teacher
with the tip of two fingers
and tell terrific tales
of Tara and Tia talking
when teacher was teaching
or Taylor and Todd typing
when teacher told them not to.

Timmy Tell-Tale
would thunder "I'm telling"
when Tina tickled Travis
and tell teacher he would
with the tip tap of two fingers
and a terrible tale of...

"Teacher I told them not to tickle
throughout all your teaching
and I told them I'm telling."

Timmy Tell-Tale
told so many tales
of talkers and ticklers
and tiptoeing tricksters
that teacher got so tired
of Timmy's tall tales
that when Timmy told them...

Teacher told Timmy a tale
of Timmy in **TROUBLE**!

An A* from Miss Coo

"The sun is as long as spaghetti" I said
"No" said Miss Coo "That can't be right, do it again
and do it right"

"Water is as twinkerly as the stars" I said
"No" said Miss Coo "That can't be right, do it again
and do it right"

"Clouds are fire in the night sky" I said
"No" said Miss Coo "That can't be right, do it again
and do it right"

I wrote a poem for Miss Coo's class...

"The sun is round,
water is wet,
the clouds are fluffy."

Golden time

Golden time –
jewelled minutes
and silvered seconds?

Golden time –
a diamond clock
with ruby numbers?

Golden time –
a free hour
doing what I please?

Golden time –
hands clasped on mouth
catching laughter with a new friend.

Golden time –
the inhale of breath
as the idea chimes.

Golden time –
a room of beaming faces,
every heart in sync.

School tomorrow – excuses for Mum

Back at school tomorrow.

Not tomorrow!
One more day off please.
I'm sick.
I'm not ready.
I haven't done my homework.

We don't do much the first week back.
Miss won't mind if I miss one day.
My uniform is dirty.
I can't remember where the school is.

I want to stay home with you.
We should spend more quality time together.

I need a few more days to grow up.
I won't know anyone – they'll all be older.
The school fell down during the summer.
The school has flooded.
The school ran away.
The school is still on holiday.

I can't go to school tomorrow...
My foot hurts.
My leg hurts.
My arm hurts.
My face hurts.
My belly hurts.
I have the runs.
I have heat stroke.
I have the plague!

I'll stay home and clean and cook.
I'll pay the bills,
sort out the tax,
handle the builders,
get the shopping.
I won't see my friends.
I'll miss that topic about the Romans.
I won't find out my results.
I won't get to laugh in assembly,
or joke with Mr Lindon.
I won't play football.
I won't make a circuit.
Or get to quote Shakespeare...

Where's my uniform?

Signed by a snail

In a landscape of poster paint
they gather in the centre,
their droppings betraying their route.
Black at the tank I left open,
multi-coloured in the pile of artworks
where Miss Irwin found them.

Their wet mouths have premasticated the edges,
digested holes in mini Pollocks,
chewed over the next Rothko,
re-arranged a Picasso-in-waiting.

Full and sated they retract.
A herd huddled in Year 4's work.
Silvered slime trails webbing the brush strokes.
Each painting graffiti'd in the course of a night.
Signed by a snail.

Gingerbread man

Billy chased me round the playground
with hands full of fists.

Billy yelled at me across the football pitch
with a mouth full of stings.

Billy spat, jibed and cawed
as I ran away singing...

"You can't catch me, I'm the gingerbread man."

Billy had red hair.
I was cruel and called him names.

Make it bigger, Eileen!

In Art I drew a park
with a pond, and railings, and children playing...
and trees with multi-coloured leaves
and mothers with pushchairs wearing hats that jumped
and joggers running with three legs
and skaters – skating on thin ice with elephants
    on their backs
and pigeons playing cards on bread tables
and grass with eyes and noses
and flowers with walking sticks and headphones
and clouds that rained smells
and a sun as deep as an ocean
and stones that bled
and a rainbow with stairs.

Sir said...

"Tut, tut, tut. Bigger, Eileen,
your picture must be bigger."

So I drew a duck.

Aardvark

I know an aardvark.
He works in a prison
as a guardvark.

He spends his whole day
walking round the yardvark.

The work's not easy,
it's very hardvark.

I am a writer

I am the clash and collide of the stars
because I create worlds.

I am the awareness of the trees
because I hear the wind.

I am the sweat of a rainbow
because I refract all colours.

I am the blood in a pen
because I ink arteries.

I am the blade in a sharpener
because I make nibs vanish.

I am the edge of a rubber,
rounded, worn and softened by mistakes.

I am the conversation of notes,
discussing melodies.

I am the holes in a flute,
knower of unknown tunes.

I am the skin of a drum.
Every hit, beat and bang
bouncing off me,
forming music from nothing.

M.O.R.E.R.A.P.S.

The **M.O.R.E.R.A.P.S.** are a trick
to help with your writing.
They add a kick to language.
Make writing more exciting.

M is for Metaphor –
saying one thing IS another.
"The sun is an oven."
"The Earth is everyone's mother."

O is for Onomatopoeia –
words that are also sounds.
"*Whoosh* went the wind."
"*Howl* went the hound."

R is for Rhyme –
words that sound the same.
You can put a cat in a hat.
Or simply try rhyming your name.

E is for Emotion –
happy, worried and sad.
Great writing shares a feeling
from the good to the bad.

R is for Repetition –
but don't repeat any old word!
Find a phrase with a musical rhythm
that sounds like a song from a bird.

A is for Alliteration –
words sharing the same starting letter,
used in the tongue-twister
that made Betty's bitter batter better.

P is for Personification –
human features ascribed to a thing.
I looked to the sky and saw
the sun's bright shining grin.

S is for Simile –
using 'as' and 'like' to compare.
For instance, "When Mother gets angry
she snarls like a rampaging bear."

The **M.O.R.E.R.A.P.S.** are a wonderful way
to add a punch to your writing.
Master them like a juggler.
Make your words ripe for the biting.

MOOOOOnomatopoeia

Hotdogs

I've never seen a hotdog.

I've seen a sausage dog
run amok in mash
and go crazy in gravy.

I've seen a bulldog
with furry horns
grazing on grass.

I've seen a sheepdog
that barks and bleats
as it makes jumpers from stinky wool.

But I've never seen a hotdog.

I've seen dog-ears in books
that flap as you read
and prick up at the scary parts.

I've seen dog-days
with lapping suns
and woofing winds.

But I've never seen a hotdog.

Do they run on coal?
And bark hot air?
Do they fan with their tails?
Do they set alight their leads?

No, I've never seen a hotdog.

Phases of phrases

Sleep on a bed of roses.
Life is good!

The coast is clear.
I'm gonna be bad!

A close shave!
I nearly got caught!

A piece of cake.
It's too easy!

Walls have ears.
People talk.

A little birdie told me.
Someone tells!

I have a bone to pick with you!
I'm in trouble!

A wolf in sheep's clothing.
My nice teacher gets angry!

Sleep on a bed of thorns.
Life is bad!

The pen is mightier than the sword.
The pen is mightier than the sword.
The pen is mightier than the sword.
I learn a lesson.

Turn over a new leaf.
I start again.

Rise from the ashes like a phoenix.
I survive.

Over the moon.
Very very
very happy!

Animal boy

Miss put me in the corner for crying crocodile tears
but my tears never bit anyone.

Sir gave me detention for being pig-headed
but I've never squealed.

I was sent to Year One for being a cheeky monkey
but I've got no fur.

The boys in class called me a chicken
but I've never laid an egg.

The girls in class called me a baboon
but my bottom is not red!

Didgeridoo

Lots of spit
and vibrating lips
come from playing a Didgeridoo.

Dingo barks
and Kookaburra harks
emerge like ghosts from this sound canoe.

Ba ba ba
and wa wa wa wa,
dreamtime sounds from a pipe of bamboo.

Deep base moans
and massaging drones
lay kisses of tones like morning dew.

Drawing

Paperclip tracing paper
over favourite picture-book page.
Sharpen the nib to nothingness.
Press with the weight of a gasp.

Whisper the tip over the tundra.
Let the lead run:
a scratching black stream
flowing into forms, pooling into shades.
An eye, a back curve, a horizon.

Migrate the sound-pouring voice to other
landscapes.
A word bubble, the pillow curve of letters,
the sought-after full-stop.

Bend the mist of tracing paper over,
reveal the original ink.
Compare it to your lead work,
search out missing lines, forgotten shades,
hidden marks...

Trace.

Copy.

Change.

Add.

Rub out.

Draw.

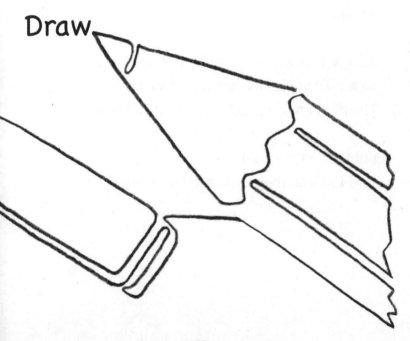

Bubble writing

Bubbled letters float.
Rounded swells speaking stars,
rainbow sheens swimming in whisper-thin skins.
Lifespans like raindrops,
like vibrations on tongues.

An **A** ascends, tilts its roof as it rises.
An **i** isochronally spins around its dot,
slipping into the curving hug of an **r**'s grasp.

The bubbled letters form words,
an alphabet aerial array.

A large **P** pogos up the ladder of an **E**,
an **a** rolls apple-like down an **r**'s kick.
The right angle of an **l** softens into a bend.

Bubbled letters float.
Two **Ps** flank the wet-burst wisp of an **O**.

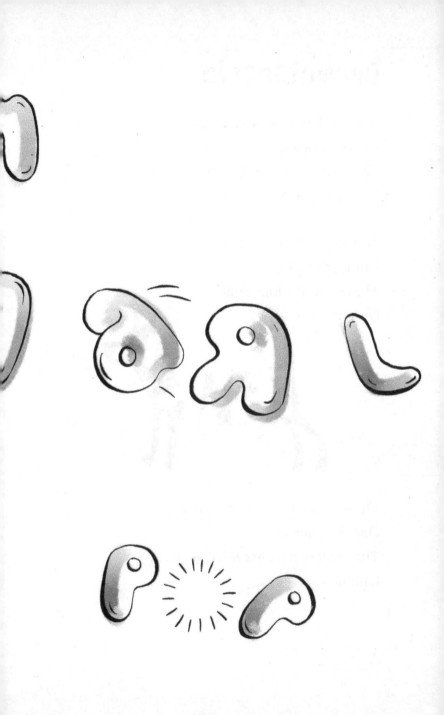

Onomatopoeia

A word that's a sound! That's...
Onomatopoeia!
The boom in a cloud! That's...
Onomatopoeia!

The bark of a dog! That's...
Onomatopoeia!
The creak of a log! That's...
Onomatopoeia!

The whoosh of a breeze! That's...
Onomatopoeia!
The atchoo of a sneeze! That's...
Onomatopoeia!

The ring of a bell! That's...
Onomatopoeia!
The splash of a well! That's...
Onomatopoeia!

The tweet of a bird! That's...
Onomatopoeia!
A sound that's a word! That's...
Onomatopoeia!

Byron hates water

Byron moved through water
like he was treading on snail shells,
like the surface could crack,
like the tinkles laughed and pointed and stared.

Byron moved through waves
like they bit,
like the ripples burned,
like the waters could swallow him.

Byron clamped his eyes against the spray,
twisted his hands into fists in the ebbs,
breathed in the mists
screamed at the flows until his fears were drowned.

A light shone at his feet
and it was all right.
Bubbles plinked by his ears
and they were all right.

Byron cupped water into his mouth
and found he could sing.
Rubbed splashes into his eyes
and saw rhythms.

Byron is dancing through deluges
in a sponge suit
with a starfish helmet.
Byron is beaming.

Byron is swaying in gushes
on a lido of pops
with an orange straw between his teeth.
Byron is giggling.

Byron is splashing the tension
with bladed hands,
with needled limbs,
with a gnashing, grinning, guffawing mouth.

Byron is laughing.

I hate spiders

I hate spiders
with their legs like spines,
bodies like drops of madness,
their webs as inescapable as a maze of
torn net curtains.

One day I lost my grandmother's ring,
the one she gave me years ago.
A special ring with a black bead centre
and diamonds like silk.

Then I saw it hanging gingerly in a spider's web
right over my bed
as if placed for me to find.

I love spiders
with their legs like my grandmother's
   knitting needles,
bodies like the beautiful black pearls that
   hung around her neck.
Their webs as cocooning as a grandmother's
   last hug.

Collective pool nouns

A *school* of pools
A *loud* of bubbles
A *soak* of splashes
A *jar* of drips
A *shower* of drips
A *curtain* of showers
A *slap* of splashes
A *bowl* of squirts
A *sliver* of splurts
A *splurge* of bursts
A *pipe* of hoots
A *splat* of splashes
A *pit-a-patter* of splatter
A *whoop* of whooshes

Skateboarding

A frozen storm-wave.
The skateboard, wide, solid and grey.

A snarling shark painted on it.

The skateboard's tips curved up,
like a rising tide
where sandy non-slip patches
clung to your feet.

We never stood,
too scared of going too deep.

Mark and I knelt on our skateboards
at the top of our whale-road,
our knees bumpy with the imprint of sand,
our hands gripped to the edges,
salt-white with anticipation.

With a surge we'd launch ourselves down.
The *thud thud thud* of the vinyl wheels
skipping over the crests of the paving joints.
The creak of the axles
as we wobbled, sea-sick on our skateboards.
The eye of the wind behind us,
we surfed between grass and road.

Feeling the rush of sea air,
imagining ourselves soaked,
toppling and rolling,
wrecked and laughing,
beached on our boards
at the world's end of our road,
our hearts a rushing tide
to meet our laughter.

Red ruby rings

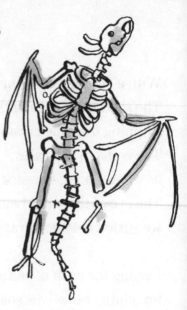

I crept along the ribs
of a sea dragon's skeleton.
I ran through the fronds
of an underwater forest.

I climbed up the ridges
of a giant crab's claws.
I clung to the feathers
of a pink albatross.

I skipped along the crests
of the crashing blue waves.
I sneaked through the cabins
of a pirate's dark ship.

I prised open the lock
of the dowager's chest.
I slipped on three rings
of the deepest ruby red.

I hid amongst the skeletons
dangling in the dungeon.
I slid down the rope
tied to the barnacled anchor.

I held on to the fin
of the breaching whale-shark.
I rolled in the surf
of the whispering tide.

I crawled along the rocks
of the boat graveyard beach.
I undid the clasps
of my three red ruby rings.

And....

Cards dealt

Dada taught me cards.
Sitting in his suit of pants and vest.
A fistful of joker-red hair strewn across his brow.
His big belly like a cannon ball.

He taught me how to shuffle cards
the way he did in American restaurants,
in bubble-filled kitchens where eyes studied
your palms.

He taught me the rules of the Rummy he played
on world-traversing ships,
cards, sea-sprayed and wind-crumpled,
slapped onto crates and pinched in sore fingers.

He taught me how to play Patience alone,
like he did in Indian cafes.
Flies landing on the chai-stained deck
as he shovelled the dirt from his long nails.

He taught me how to hold all my cards to my heart,
how to use my clubs,
spend my diamonds,
work my spades.
His huge weathered hands
dealing their skill into mine.

What do monkeys do?

If lions lie
and tigers tie
and cheetahs cheat...
what do monkeys do?

If lions tell you their tails are pink
and tigers tie knots
into their bedsheets
and cheetahs stash poker cards
under each of their feet...
what do monkeys do?

If whales wail
and hippos hip and hop
and panda's pan for gold...
what do monkeys do?

If whales cry big salty tears
and hippos wear diamonds
in each of their ears
and pandas search for gold
for years and years...
what do monkeys do?

If rats a-rat-a-tat-tat
and spiders spy
and millipedes are millionaires...
what do monkeys do?

If rats wear glasses
in low down clubs
and spiders peer
through binoculars at their grub
and millipedes count their millions
in their bath tubs...
what do monkeys do?

What do monkeys do?

The Satyr's head

The hidden garden we played in
was bordered in red brick.
Crenellations of a faded fort,
ivy-scarred and wind-aged.
A Victorian garden.

The towering walls tempted us to climb,
the bricks testing their mortar,
forming steps and hand-holds.

We climbed.
Urging frail frames against the height,
then daring to drop to the spiky grass below.
Protected by a wisp of arrogance,
an armour of childhood.

We danced in the light of the Satyr's grin,
the limestone detail of the fountain,
weathered and mean,
the endless grimace of a fiend.

The garden cloaked our tower block's stares,
its trees veiling the aerials, the satellite dishes.
Its bricks a smoke screen to the traffic's roar,
the yells of our mothers.
Its bushes covering up the smog.
The jam-sweet scent of winter berries
disguising the stench from the bins.

We danced like our fathers told us we could,
spinning in the dead leaves
that spun from our steps,
like wry circus performers.

Werewolf Club rules

Do not talk about Werewolf Club!
You can howl about it,
but never talk!

Do not walk to Werewolf Club!
You can bound to it in moonlight,
but never walk!

Do not eat sweets at Werewolf Club!
You can eat meat, raw meat,
but no sweets!

Do not bring cats to Werewolf Club!
You can bring bats, hats, and even rats,
but no cats!

Do not bring silver to Werewolf Club!
You can bring gold or pewter or even bronze,
but no silver!

Do not bring chewy toys to Werewolf Club!

If you do they will be confiscated.

You won't get them back.

They are very squeaky
and make it hard
for us to hear the day's agenda!

If all the world were paper

If all the world were paper
I would fold up my gran
and take her everywhere I go.
I would laminate my baby sister in bubble wrap
and lay her to sleep in unbound fairy-tale book pages.
And should she get scared,
rip every fear,
shred every scream,
tear every tear.

If all the world were paper
I would re-bind my grandfather,
smooth out the dog-ears to all his stories,
place his younger days in a zoetrope
and flush the harrowing chapters
down an ink-gurgling well.

If all the world were paper
kind deeds would be post-it notes
that stick to the doer in ever-growing trails,
so we would always remember,
friends would come with perforated lines
so you could keep their best bits with you
at all times.

If all the world were paper
Christmas wrapping foil and birthday cards
would follow you to school.

If all the world were paper
dreams would be braille
so we could read them whilst we slept,
nightmares would be shopping lists
because shopping lists are so easy to forget.

If all the world were paper
arguments would rustle before they started
and could be put right with a little tape.

If all the world were paper
we could paperclip families together,
draw smiles on all the sad faces,
rub out the tears,
cover our homes in Tippex and start all over again.

All the world is not paper,
but whilst we can imagine it were
we can recycle the rough times
knowing we will never ever fold.

Last day of school

Come back taller
Come back with a recipe
Come back stronger
Come back with a story

Come back with something found
Come back with a new word
Come back and astound
Come back with the song of a bird

Come back with a friend
Come back telling a joke
Come back with a new trend
Come back with a thing fixed that was broke

Come back with a beaten fear
Come back knowing a star
Come back with a sphere
Come back with stuff in a jar

Come back with a leaf
Come back pondering a query
Come back with a new belief
Come back spelling out a theory

Come back with a new taste
Come back smelling a pine cone
Come back with something traced
Come back proud at how you have grown.

JOSEPH COELHO is a performance poet and playwright. He has written plays for the Polka Theatre, the Lyric, Hammersmith, and the Unicorn Theatre. He performs his poetry shows with the UK's top performance poetry organisation, Apples and Snakes, visiting venues across the UK. Joseph's poems have appeared in many anthologies, including *Green Glass Beads* by Jacqueline Wilson and *The Works 6*, edited by Pie Corbett, but *Werewolf Club Rules* is his first solo collection. He lives in Folkestone, Kent.

MORE GREAT POETRY FROM
FRANCES LINCOLN CHILDREN'S BOOKS

978-1-84780-365-8

Shortlisted for the CLPE Poetry Prize 2014

'Lovely to read aloud with catchy rhymes and topics
guaranteed to appeal to children. The language is vivid
and some of the poems end in an unexpected way that
will make children giggle.' – *Parents in Touch*

978-1-84780-398-6

Shortlisted for the CLPE Poetry Prize 2014

'Award-winning Grace Nichols creates all the moods
evoked by the title in this beautiful anthology which
lightly captures the wonder of the world ... Every
poem is a delight in itself while together they give
readers a newly painted world.' – *Love Reading*